52 DIY CRAFTS for Girls

Whitney + Westleigh
-with-
KARIANNE WOOD

Illustrations by Michal Sparks

HARVEST kids

HARVEST HOUSE PUBLISHERS
EUGENE, OREGON

CONTENTS

STUFF YOU CAN MAKE FOR
Yourself

STUFF YOU CAN MAKE FOR
Your Friends

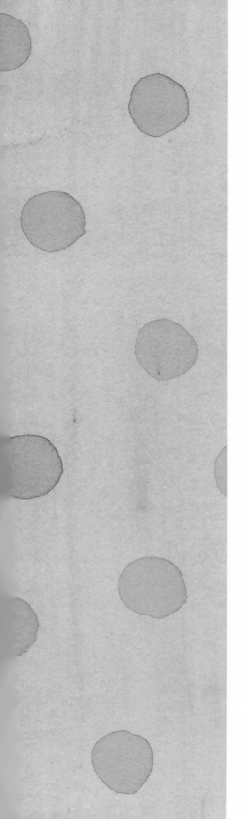

STUFF YOU CAN MAKE FOR
Your Family

STUFF YOU CAN MAKE FOR
Your Room

STUFF YOU CAN MAKE FOR
Your Locker

STUFF YOU CAN MAKE FOR
Your Party

STUFF YOU CAN MAKE FOR
Valentine's Day

STUFF YOU CAN MAKE FOR
Easter

STUFF YOU CAN MAKE FOR
the Fourth of July

STUFF YOU CAN MAKE FOR
Thanksgiving

STUFF YOU CAN MAKE FOR
Christmas

Hello!

Do you like crafting? Do you like making things? Do you like giving gifts to your friends? Do you like glitter and paint and banners and parties and decorating your room?

Oh, good.

We do too.

We're Whitney and Westleigh. We're twins who live in Texas with our mom and dad, our brothers, and our golden retriever, Buddy. We've been making and creating and drawing and painting for as long as we can remember, and we're so excited to share this book of some of our favorite projects with you.

But before we start creating together, here's a little more about us.

I'm Westleigh. I'm older than my sister by one minute. I know it's only a minute, but it's a very important one. I love to watch romantic comedies. I love "happily ever afters." I love popcorn and ranch dressing and strawberries and smoothies. I love calligraphy and handwritten anything. And I love Jesus. I love Him more than bagel bites—and that's a lot.

I'm Whitney. I'm the younger sister. Just in case I ever forget I'm younger, Westleigh reminds me. I love encouraging other people. I love my family, and I love it when Buddy takes me for a walk. I love flowers. I love macaroni and cheese with hot dogs. I love dancing and twirling and spinning through life. And I love Jesus and Post-it notes (in that order).

And the best part?

We get to craft with *you*. We've designed projects you can make in an afternoon. There's stuff for your locker and stuff for your friends and stuff for your family and stuff for your room and stuff you can make just for you.

We know we've just met, but we can already tell that you are amazing.

And wonderful.

And special.

And incredible. And creative and funny and joyful and full of life.

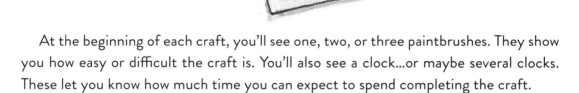

Let's be friends.

At the beginning of each craft, you'll see one, two, or three paintbrushes. They show you how easy or difficult the craft is. You'll also see a clock...or maybe several clocks. These let you know how much time you can expect to spend completing the craft.

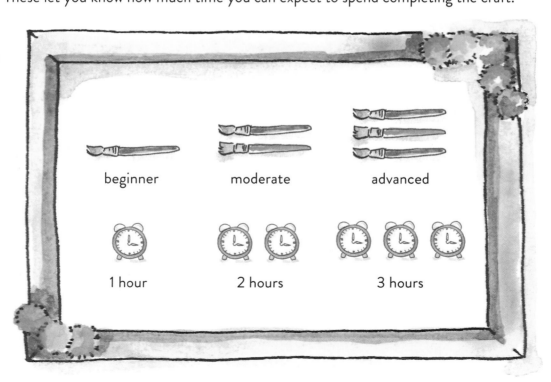

beginner   moderate   advanced

1 hour   2 hours   3 hours

STUFF YOU CAN
MAKE FOR

Yourself

DIY FLOWER PEN

SKILL LEVEL

TIME

SUPPLIES

- ☐ large silk daisy
- ☐ ballpoint pen
- ☐ glue
- ☐ washi tape

INSTRUCTIONS

1. Remove the daisy from the stem.

2. Glue the daisy to the top of the pen.

3. Let dry.

4. Wrap the entire pen and the bottom of the flower with washi tape.

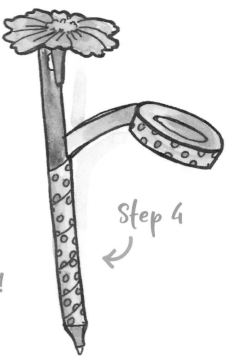

Step 4

All done!

Westleigh Says...
You can use washi tape instead of floral tape to add a pattern.

Whitney Says...
You can glue a pom-pom to the top instead of a daisy.

MONOGRAMMED FLOWERPOT

SKILL LEVEL

TIME

SUPPLIES

- [ ] terra-cotta pot
- [ ] large printout of a single-letter monogram
- [ ] graphite paper
- [ ] pencil
- [ ] white craft paint
- [ ] gold craft paint

Finished!

INSTRUCTIONS

1. Paint the entire terra-cotta pot with white craft paint.

2. Let dry.

3. Check to see if the pot needs a second coat. If it does, paint a second coat on the pot and let it dry.

4. Trace the letter onto the pot with graphite paper.

5. Fill in the outline of the entire letter with gold paint.

6. Let dry.

7. Plant one of your favorite plants inside and decorate your room.

Step 1

Step 4

Step 5

Westleigh Says...

Succulents are my favorite plants.

Whitney Says...

I just love flowers—any kind.

POM-POM BOOKMARK

SKILL LEVEL

TIME

SUPPLIES

- [ ] yarn
- [ ] cardboard
- [ ] fabric glue
- [ ] ribbon

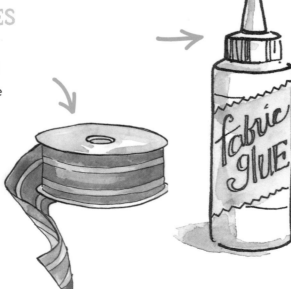

INSTRUCTIONS

1. We are all about pom-poms here and use them for so many different crafts. Turn to page 137 to learn how to make them.

2. Choose a color of yarn that looks good with the color you choose for your bookmark ribbon.

3. Follow the instructions on page 137 to make 2 small pom-poms. Use 3-inch pieces of cardboard.

4. Leave the string on the pom-poms when you tie them off.

5. Cut a length of ribbon 12 inches long.

6. Fold over each end of the ribbon and glue a loop on each end.

7. Let dry.

8. Tie a pom-pom through the loop on each end of the ribbon.

9. Make different bookmarks in different colors and decorate your bookshelf!

Step 6

Step 8

Done!

4

SCRIPTURE MAGNETS

SKILL LEVEL

TIME

SUPPLIES

- ☐ printed Scripture verses
- ☐ Mod Podge
- ☐ glass stones
- ☐ magnets
- ☐ glue

Westleigh Says...

You can mix it up a little by using scrapbook paper instead.

Whitney Says...

If the Scripture verse is too long, you can always just write the Scripture reference instead.

INSTRUCTIONS

1. Print some of your favorite Scripture verses from a computer in a tiny (8-point) font.

2. Place a glass stone over the Scripture verses to make sure the printouts are the right size.

3. Trace a circle around the Scripture verse the size of the glass stone.

4. Cut out the circle.

5. Paint a small amount of Mod Podge over the front of the Scripture verse and stick it to the back of the stone. (Turn to page 140 to learn how to use Mod Podge.)

6. Let dry.

7. Glue a magnet to the back of the stone.

8. Your magnets are ready to use for decorating.

Step 4 →

Step 5

Step 7

Finito!

FLEECE PILLOW

SKILL LEVEL

TIME

SUPPLIES

- [ ] 2 contrasting yards of fleece
- [ ] scissors
- [ ] 20 by 20-inch pillow form

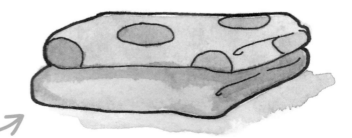

INSTRUCTIONS

1. Cut a 28 by 28-inch square of fleece from each yard of fabric.

2. Cut a 6 by 6-inch square from each of the four corners of the fabric.

3. Cut fringes around the outside of each of the fabric squares. Each piece of fringe should measure 2 inches wide and 6 inches long. Continue cutting until you have cut a fringe on all 4 sides of each of the squares of fabric.

4. Place the pillow form in the center of one piece of fabric. Lay the other piece of fabric over the pillow form.

5. Using the fringe pieces, tie the squares of fabric together at the corners.

6. Tie the fringe pieces together along each side.

7. Fluff your pillow. It's ready to use to decorate.

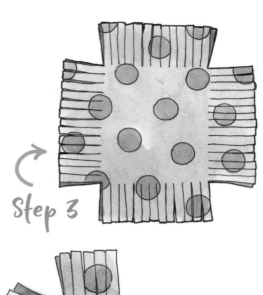

Step 3

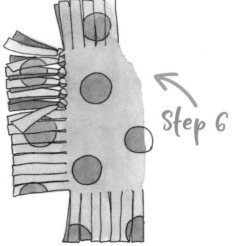

Step 6

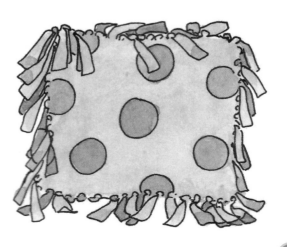

Too cute!

STUFF YOU CAN
MAKE FOR

Your Friends

BEAD AND TASSEL GARLAND

SKILL LEVEL

TIME

SUPPLIES

- [ ] 50 wood beads
- [ ] jute twine
- [ ] cream-colored chunky knit yarn
- [ ] scissors
- [ ] cardboard

All done!

INSTRUCTIONS

1. Cut a piece of jute twine 36 inches long.

2. Tie one bead onto the end of the twine. Tie a double knot 3 inches from the end of the twine to secure the beads.

3. String the rest of the beads onto the twine.

4. Tie off the last bead on the strand. Tie a double knot 3 inches from the end of the twine to secure the beads.

5. Make 2 tassels by following the instructions on page 138.

6. Tie a tassel to one end of the garland.

7. Repeat for the second tassel.

Step 3

Step 5

Westleigh Says...

You can change out the color of the tassels to match your friend's room.

Whitney Says...

You could tie pom-poms to the ends of the garland instead of tassels.

WASHI-TAPE HAIR ACCESSORIES

SKILL LEVEL

TIME

SUPPLIES

- ☐ dollar-store barrettes
- ☐ washi tape
- ☐ cardboard
- ☐ hole punch

INSTRUCTIONS

1. Remove a barrette from the store packaging and lay it flat.

2. Wrap the barrette with washi tape, starting at one end.

3. Cut out a 4 by 6-inch piece of cardboard.

4. Punch 2 holes in the cardboard to attach the barrette.

5. Place the barrette in the cardboard and clip it closed.

6. Decorate the front of the cardboard with your friend's name.

Step 1

Step 2

Step 5

HAND-STITCHED NOTEBOOK

SKILL LEVEL

TIME

SUPPLIES

- [ ] small notebook with a paper cover
- [ ] embroidery thread
- [ ] embroidery needle

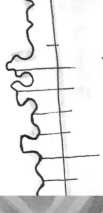

Westleigh says...

You could also draw your friend's name and stitch that instead of a design.

Whitney says...

Make sure to write a welcome message to them on the inside cover.

INSTRUCTIONS

1. Lightly sketch a design you like on the notebook cover with a pencil. (Or using carbon paper, trace the one we created for you on page 141).

2. Thread the embroidery needle.

3. Stitch along the drawn pencil line with your needle and thread. Look on pages 134–136 for several different types of stitches you can use. The backstitch is our favorite.

4. When your thread runs out, tie a knot and rethread the needle.

5. Keep stitching until all your pencil lines are covered with stitches.

Step 2

Step 3

Voilà!

52 THINGS I LIKE ABOUT YOU

SKILL LEVEL

TIME

SUPPLIES

- ☐ 52 blank 3 by 5-inch cards
- ☐ hole punch
- ☐ markers
- ☐ jump ring

Westleigh says...

Here are some of my favorite friend words: awesome, incredible, amazing, smart, and funny.

Whitney says...

Here are some of my favorite friend words: sweet, kind, nice, thoughtful, considerate, and friendly.

INSTRUCTIONS

1. Use the marker to write "52 Things I Like About You" on one card. On the back of the card, write one thing you like about your friend.

2. Write one thing you like about your friend on each of the rest of the cards. Feel free to decorate! Leave the back of each card blank.

3. Punch a hole in the top left corner of each card.

4. Open the jump ring and add the cards to the ring through the holes. Add the cover card last.

5. Close the jump ring, and your gift is ready to give.

Step 2

funny Smart nice Kind

Like it!

FELT MONOGRAMMED GIFT-CARD HOLDER

SKILL LEVEL

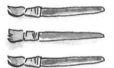

TIME

↳ Ready!

SUPPLIES

- ☐ felt
- ☐ embroidery thread in contrasting colors
- ☐ embroidery needle
- ☐ wood letter (the first letter of your friend's first name)
- ☐ fabric glue

INSTRUCTIONS

Step 1

1. Cut out a piece of felt 4 by 6 inches.

2. Fold the piece of felt in half.

3. Using a blanket stitch (see note on page 136), stitch the sides of the felt closed as shown, leaving the top open.

4. Using fabric glue, glue the letter onto the front of the holder.

5. Place a gift card inside the holder. Your gift is ready to give!

Step 3

Step 4

STUFF YOU CAN MAKE FOR

Your Family

FAMILY QUOTE WALL

SKILL LEVEL

TIME

SUPPLIES

- [ ] four 8 by 10-inch picture frames
- [ ] 4 favorite family quotes
- [ ] 5 by 7-inch white cardstock
- [ ] Sharpie

INSTRUCTIONS

1. Talk with your family and choose 4 favorite things your family members often say.

2. Write each saying on a piece of cardstock with the Sharpie.

3. Open the frames and insert the quote between the 2 pieces of glass.

4. Close the frames and hang them near each other to create a family quote wall.

"Rise & Shine & give GOD the glory glory."

Voilà! ↗

Westleigh says...

One of my favorite family sayings is "Rise and shine and give God the glory."

Whitney says...

You can also choose your favorite Scripture verses.

FLORAL PICTURE-FRAME WREATH

SKILL LEVEL

TIME

SUPPLIES

- ☐ 11 by 13-inch plain picture frame without glass or backing
- ☐ large flowers
- ☐ medium flowers (preferably ones with a different texture)
- ☐ smaller flowers (preferably ones in a different color)
- ☐ tiny flowers (preferably ones that drape a little)
- ☐ craft glue
- ☐ ribbon

Lovely!

INSTRUCTIONS

1. Remove the stems from the flowers. They should pull right off.

2. Glue the largest flower to a corner of the frame.

3. Glue a medium flower on either side.

4. Continue alternating the different types of flowers until you have covered the corner of the frame and about 8 inches on each side.

5. Stand back and check to see if you need to add any more flowers.

6. Once your wreath is finished, add a ribbon to hang it on your door or wall.

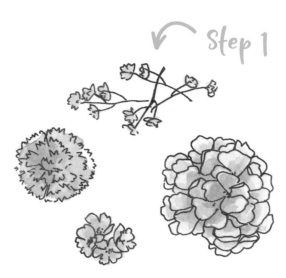

Step 1

Step 2

PERSONALIZED FAMILY RIBBON

SKILL LEVEL

TIME

SUPPLIES

- ☐ loose-weave 3-inch burlap ribbon
- ☐ your family name printed on white paper
- ☐ Sharpie

Westleigh says...
You can tie your family ribbon on a wreath.

Whitney says...
You can add it to picture frames too.

INSTRUCTIONS

1. Print out your family name on white printer paper. Choose a pretty font and print it at 75-point size.

2. Place your family name under the burlap ribbon so you can see it through the ribbon. Line it up so it's centered on the ribbon.

3. Trace the name of your family onto the ribbon with a Sharpie.

4. Repeat steps 2 and 3 until you have the length of ribbon you want.

5. Cut the ribbon. It's ready to decorate with.

Step 1

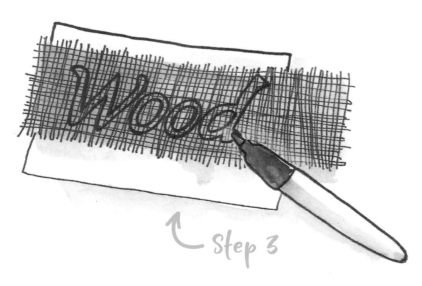

Step 3

SCRABBLE-TILE FAMILY-NAME PROJECT

SKILL LEVEL

TIME

SUPPLIES

- [ ] Scrabble tiles
- [ ] Scrabble tile holder
- [ ] glue

INSTRUCTIONS

1. Find the Scrabble tiles that spell out your family name.

2. Place them in order on the Scrabble tile holder.

3. Glue them in place. Your Scrabble tile holder is ready to decorate with.

All done!

Westleigh says...
My mom and I often find Scrabble games at yard sales.

Whitney says...
You can also find just the tiles and the holder in the scrapbook section of most craft stores.

15

FAMILY-NAME ROPE ART

SKILL LEVEL

TIME

SUPPLIES

- [ ] 8 by 4-inch wood plaque
- [ ] graphite paper (or carbon paper)
- [ ] pencil
- [ ] rope
- [ ] craft glue

Fun!

INSTRUCTIONS

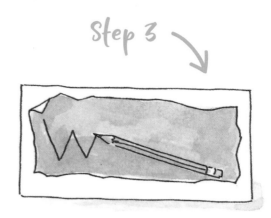

Step 3

1. Print out your family name from a computer in a cursive font with a 200-point size. You may need to print it on different pages. That's okay—you can just cut the letters to fit.

2. Lay a piece of graphite paper over the wood plaque, and then place your family's name over the graphite paper.

3. Trace the name onto the wood using a pencil. The graphite paper will transfer the name onto the wood.

Step 4

4. After you've finished tracing the name, next trace the name with craft glue.

5. Start at one end of the name and place the rope on the glue, following the outline of your family's name.

6. Keep placing the rope on the glue until you have filled in the name.

Step 5

7. Let dry. Your name art is ready to decorate with.

STUFF YOU CAN MAKE FOR

Your Room

PERSONALIZED SCRIPTURE CLIPBOARD

SKILL LEVEL

TIME

SUPPLIES

- [ ] plain clipboard
- [ ] 2 coordinating colors of craft paint
- [ ] painter's tape
- [ ] chalk
- [ ] piece of white paper
- [ ] paintbrush
- [ ] ribbon
- [ ] scissors
- [ ] favorite Scripture verse

← Voilà!

INSTRUCTIONS

1. Tape a rectangle at the bottom of the clipboard with the painter's tape.

2. Paint the inside of the rectangle with one of the colors of craft paint.

3. Let dry. If necessary, paint a second coat and let it dry.

4. Use the chalk to write your name at the bottom of the clipboard. Have fun. Don't worry about it being perfect. This is your clipboard for your room. Just write your name in your own handwriting.

5. Using the second color of craft paint, paint over the chalk writing.

6. Tie a bow with ribbon on the top of the clipboard.

7. Print your favorite Scripture verse from a computer.

8. Clip it onto the clipboard. Place the clipboard on your desk or bookshelf or dresser and change the Scripture verse whenever you like.

Step 2

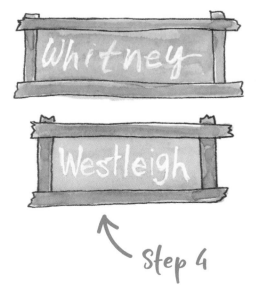

Step 4

POM-POM THROW

SKILL LEVEL

TIME

SUPPLIES

- [ ] store-bought throw with a loose weave
- [ ] yarn
- [ ] 5-inch square piece of cardboard

Cozy!

INSTRUCTIONS

1. We are all about pom-poms here and use them for so many different crafts. Turn to page 137 to learn how to make them.

2. Choose a yarn color that goes well with the color of the store-bought blanket you will be using for this project.

3. Follow the instructions on page 137 to make approximately 24 large pom-poms using a 5-inch piece of cardboard.

4. When making the pom-poms, make sure to leave extra yarn when you tie off the pom-pom in the middle.

5. When you've made all the pom-poms, lay the throw flat on the floor. Pull the weave slightly apart at one corner. Tie the strings of a pom-pom onto the corner of the throw.

6. Repeat for each of the other corners of the throw.

7. Place 5 pom-poms on one side of the throw to make sure they are evenly spaced. Don't tie them yet.

8. Once you are happy with the spacing, pull the weave slightly apart and tie the pom-pom to the throw.

9. Repeat with each of the other 3 sides. Your throw is ready—toss it on the bed or over a chair in your room!

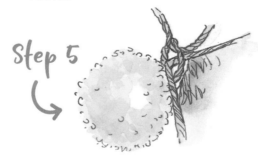

Step 5

Step 6

Step 7

18

POLKA-DOT PAINTED CLOTHESPIN PHOTO DISPLAY

SKILL LEVEL

TIME

SUPPLIES

- [ ] 2 coordinating colors of craft paint
- [ ] paintbrushes
- [ ] plain clothespins
- [ ] Q-tips
- [ ] jute twine

cute! ↗

INSTRUCTIONS

1. Paint the tops of the clothespins in different colors. Choose colors that make you happy and match your room.

2. Let dry.

3. Flip the clothespins over and paint a different color on the reverse side.

4. Let dry.

5. Dip the Q-tip in the coordinating paint color and add polka dots to your clothespins.

6. Let dry.

7. Cut a piece of twine 1 yard long. Tie off loops on the ends of the twine. Have your parents nail 2 nails into the wall and attach the loops of the string onto the nails.

8. Clip your favorite photos onto the string with your polka-dot clothespins.

Step 1

Step 5

Whitney says...
I painted mine navy and yellow.

Westleigh says...
I painted mine blush and gold.

19

DECORATIVE MONOGRAM

SKILL LEVEL

TIME

SUPPLIES

- [ ] 1 craft-paper letter (try the first letter of your first or last name)
- [ ] scrapbook paper
- [ ] scissors
- [ ] Mod Podge
- [ ] 2 by 4 by 6-inch piece of wood
- [ ] acrylic craft paint
- [ ] small paintbrush
- [ ] glue

Finished!

INSTRUCTIONS

1. Cut out ten 3 by 3-inch squares of different patterns of scrapbook paper. Cut out seven 2 by 2-inch squares of scrapbook paper.

Step 1

2. Apply the larger squares of different patterns to the craft letter with Mod Podge. (Turn to page 140 to learn how to use Mod Podge.)

Step 2

3. Let dry.

4. Fill in the holes on the letter with the smaller squares of different patterns of scrapbook paper.

5. Let dry.

6. Paint the piece of wood with craft paint to compliment the scrapbook paper.

Step 8

7. Let dry.

8. Glue the letter to the piece of wood.

9. Your monogram is ready to decorate with.

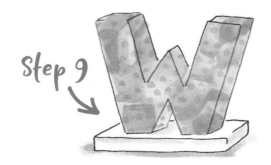

Step 9

53

20

SCRIPTURE ROCKS

SKILL LEVEL

TIME

SUPPLIES

- ☐ rocks (you can collect these from your yard or you can purchase them at a craft store)
- ☐ 4 coordinating colors of craft paint
- ☐ paintbrushes
- ☐ Q-tips
- ☐ acrylic sealer

Whitney says...
My favorite Scripture verse is Romans 8:1–2.

Westleigh says...
My favorite Scripture verse is Matthew 5:16.

INSTRUCTIONS

1. Paint the rocks with a base coat of craft paint.

2. Let dry.

3. Paint your favorite Scripture verse on the rocks with a thin brush and craft paint.

4. Add polka dots or arrows or doodles to finish decorating the rock.

5. Once the paint dries, coat the rock with the sealer.

6. Decorate your desk or bookshelves with the rock or give them to your friends to decorate theirs.

Step 1

Step 3

Step 4

STUFF YOU CAN MAKE FOR

Your Locker

21

MAGNETIC "STUFF" HOLDER

SKILL LEVEL

TIME

SUPPLIES

- [ ] cereal box
- [ ] contact paper
- [ ] scissors
- [ ] pen
- [ ] ruler
- [ ] white name-tag sticker
- [ ] self-adhesive magnets

Westleigh says...

I like to keep handwritten notes in mine.

Whitney says...

I like to keep homework to do in mine.

INSTRUCTIONS

Step 4

1. Clean out the inside of the cereal box. Remove the plastic wrapper. Wipe lightly with a damp towel to remove the crumbs.

2. Measure down 6 inches from the top of the box with the ruler.

3. Draw a horizontal line across the middle of the box with the pen.

4. Cut along the line with scissors, removing the top and the front part of the box.

Step 5

5. Cover the entire box with contact paper.

6. Smooth out any bubbles in the paper.

7. Attach the magnets to the back of the box.

8. Add a name-tag sticker to the front of the container and label it with "stuff."

9. Hang your "stuff" box in your locker to have a place for everything and keep everything in its place.

Step 8

22

PHOTO FRIEND MAGNETS

SKILL LEVEL

TIME

SUPPLIES

- [ ] 2 by 3-inch mini picture frame
- [ ] washi tape
- [ ] pictures
- [ ] self-adhesive magnets

INSTRUCTIONS

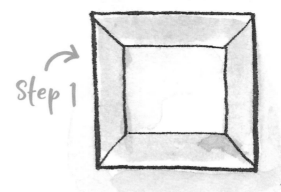

Step 1

1. Remove the back from the mini picture frame and the plastic or glass from the front, leaving only the front.

2. If there is a hanger on the back of the frame, detach it, leaving a smooth surface.

3. Wrap the frame in washi tape with your favorite pattern on it.

Step 3

4. Replace the plastic or glass in the front of the frame. Add a picture and then the smooth back with the hanger removed.

5. Attach the magnets to the back of the picture frame. Your picture frame is ready to decorate your locker.

Fun!

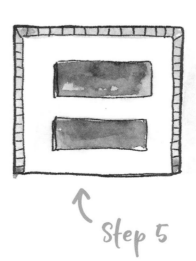

Step 5

23
CARDBOARD NOTEBOOKS

SKILL LEVEL

TIME

SUPPLIES

- ☐ two 5 by 7-inch pieces of cardboard
- ☐ scrapbook paper
- ☐ stickers
- ☐ scissors
- ☐ hole punch
- ☐ 3-inch jump rings

Westleigh says...
I like to write notes in the book.

Whitney says...
I like to keep track of my homework in the notebook.

INSTRUCTIONS

1. Lay one of the pieces of 5 by 7-inch cardboard flat on the scrapbook paper. Trace around the edges.

2. Cut out the piece of scrapbook paper.

3. Repeat until you have 25 pieces of 5 by 7-inch scrapbook paper.

4. Mark 2 holes 1½ inches from the edge of both pieces of cardboard and on all 25 pieces of scrapbook paper. Make sure all the holes are marked in the same place.

5. Hole punch through the marks. Tip: You can punch through several pieces of paper at the same time.

6. Place a piece of cardboard, then the 25 pieces of scrapbook paper, and then the second piece of cardboard together so all the holes line up.

7. Attach the jump ring through all the holes.

8. Decorate the front of the book.

Step 1

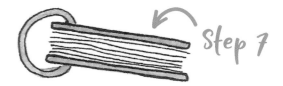

Step 3

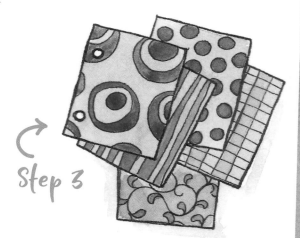

Step 7

Step 8

24

COFFEE CAN PENCIL HOLDER

SKILL LEVEL

TIME

SUPPLIES

- ☐ metal coffee can
- ☐ patterned duct tape
- ☐ pencils and pens

INSTRUCTIONS

Step 1

1. Start by washing out the coffee can. Remove all the dust and coffee grounds and let it dry thoroughly.

2. Wrap a piece of tape all the way around the coffee can at the top.

Step 2

3. Add another piece of tape under that, making sure it wraps all the way around the can.

4. Keep adding rows of tape until the entire can is covered.

5. Make sure all the tape is pressed down.

6. Place the can in the bottom of your locker and use it to organize school supplies.

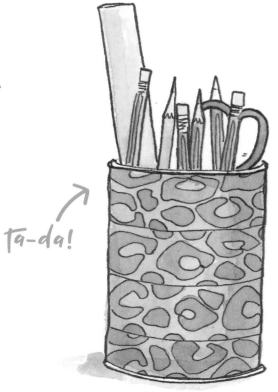

Ta-da!

25

SCRIPTURE BOOKMARKS

SKILL LEVEL

TIME

SUPPLIES

- [ ] cardstock
- [ ] Scripture verses
- [ ] clear contact paper
- [ ] scissors

Westleigh says...

If you don't want to print the verses from a computer, you can also just cut out an 8 by 3-inch piece of cardstock and write a verse on it.

Whitney says...

I like to punch a hole in the top and add a tassel.

INSTRUCTIONS

1. Make a list of your favorite Scripture verses.

2. Type them out on a computer and print them on a piece of cardstock.

3. Cut the cardstock around each Scripture verse in a rectangle. (Most of our bookmarks were about 8 inches long and 3 inches wide.)

4. Place the printed cardstock on the sticky side of a piece of clear contact paper.

5. Place another piece of contact paper on top with the 2 sticky sides together.

6. Press firmly to make sure there aren't any bubbles.

7. Cut out the bookmark from the contact paper, leaving a 1-inch border of clear contact paper around the edge.

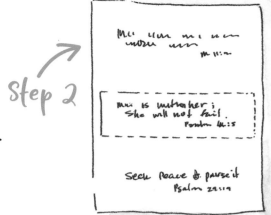

Step 2

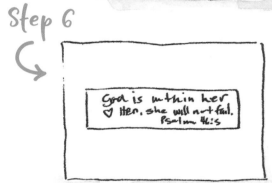

Step 6

Finito

STUFF YOU CAN MAKE FOR

Your Party

26

POM-POM PARTY HATS

SKILL LEVEL

TIME

SUPPLIES

- [ ] premade party hats
- [ ] yarn
- [ ] 3-inch piece of cardboard
- [ ] scissors
- [ ] fabric glue

INSTRUCTIONS

1. We are all about pom-poms here and use them for so many different crafts. Turn to page 137 to learn how to make them.

2. Choose a yarn color that goes well with the color of the hat.

3. Follow the instructions on page 137 to make approximately 15 small pom-poms for each hat using a 3-inch piece of cardboard.

4. Fluff and trim your pom-poms until they are round.

5. Using fabric glue, glue the pom-poms to the rim of the party hat.

6. Let dry.

7. Check to make sure all the pom-poms are glued on until they stick, and your hats are ready to party!

Step 5 →

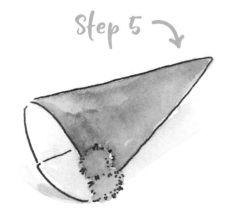

Ready! →

27

ASYMMETRICAL HULA-HOOP WREATH

SKILL LEVEL

TIME

← Adorable!

SUPPLIES

- [ ] standard-size hula hoop
- [ ] gold duct tape
- [ ] black Sharpie
- [ ] paper or silk flowers with wire stems
- [ ] greenery with wire stems
- [ ] scissors

INSTRUCTIONS

1. Wrap the gold duct tape around the hula hoop. Keep wrapping until the entire hula hoop is covered.

2. Place the hula hoop on a table. Mark 2 o'clock and 7 o'clock on the hula hoop with a black dot using the Sharpie.

3. Wire one stem of flowers near one dot. Wire one stem of greenery next to it.

4. Continue alternating flowers and greenery until you have approximately 6 inches of flowers and greenery on one side. Repeat steps 3 and 4 for the second dot.

5. Step back and assess to see if you need to add more greenery or flowers.

6. Add more greenery and flowers if needed. Fluff. Your wreath is ready to party!

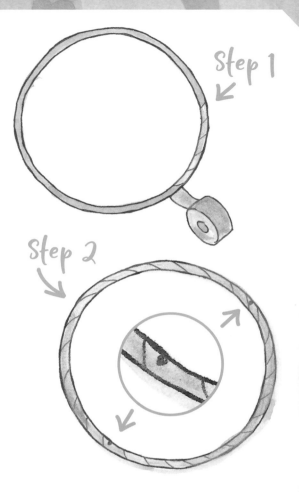

Step 1

Step 2

Step 4

28

GOLD-FOIL TREAT GARLAND

SKILL LEVEL

TIME

SUPPLIES

- [ ] empty cardboard paper-towel roll
- [ ] gold foil
- [ ] small treats and/or toys
- [ ] string
- [ ] scissors

ta-da!

INSTRUCTIONS

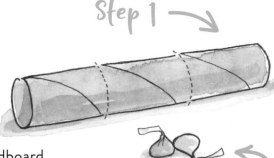

1. Cut the cardboard paper-towel rolls into 3 symmetrical pieces.

2. Place a small treat or toy inside the cardboard roll.

3. Thread the string through the cardboard roll.

4. Cut a square piece of gold foil that covers the entire cardboard roll with a 4-inch foil allowance on the ends.

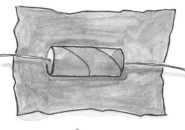

5. Wrap the piece of cardboard roll with the foil and twist the ends like a candy wrapper. Tie string to secure.

6. Using the same piece of string, add another foil-covered treat to the garland, following the instructions in steps 2 through 5. Allow 10 inches between each popper.

7. Continue adding poppers to the string until you have 12 poppers on the garland.

8. Hang up the garland at your party. When the party is finished, cut the garland apart and give each guest their own treat as a party favor.

29

COFFEE-FILTER FLOWERS

SKILL LEVEL

TIME

24 HOURS

(most of this is drying time)

SUPPLIES

- ☐ coffee filters
- ☐ craft paint
- ☐ floral tape
- ☐ Scotch tape
- ☐ floral wire
- ☐ scissors

Finished!

INSTRUCTIONS

1. Dye the coffee filters a variety of colors. Just mix 5 parts water to 1 part craft paint. Dip the coffee filters in the paint/water mixture until they absorb the color.

2. Lay the coffee filters flat until they dry. This takes a while. If it's a sunny day, place them out in the sun, where they will dry faster.

3. Cut a slit in each coffee filter from the edge to the center.

4. Roll up the edge of the coffee filter. Continue until you have rolled up the entire filter into a cone. Do not roll it too tightly—looser is better.

5. Tape the end of the cone with Scotch tape. This is the center of your flower.

6. Roll another coffee filter (dyed a different color) around the outside of the first one.

7. Pinch the ends of the 2 filters and tape them with Scotch tape again.

8. Tape a piece of floral wire to the bottom of the flower with Scotch tape.

9. Cover the bottom of the flower and stem with floral tape. Wind the tape around until it covers the wire.

10. Fluff and shape. The flower is ready to be added to a centerpiece, wound onto a wreath, or added to a garland.

30

POM-POM GARLAND

SKILL LEVEL

TIME

SUPPLIES

- ☐ yarn
- ☐ 3-inch piece of cardboard
- ☐ scissors

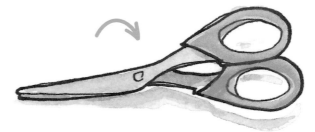

INSTRUCTIONS

1. Choose a pattern using various colors of yarn. You can alternate colors, or you can use different shades of the same color.

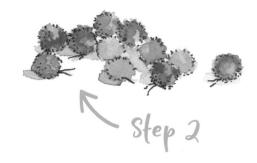

Step 2

2. Follow the instructions on page 137 to make 40 to 50 small pom-poms for your garland using the 3-inch piece of cardboard.

3. Make sure to leave extra yarn when you tie off each pom-pom in the middle. You will use this extra yarn to tie each pom-pom to the garland.

4. Cut a piece of yarn the length of the garland.

Step 5

5. Tie one pom-pom to the piece of yarn 13 inches from one end.

6. Tie the next pom-pom onto the longer side of the piece of yarn. Continue tying the pom-poms to the piece of yarn until you have the length of garland that works for your party. Your garland is ready to party!

Fun!

STUFF YOU CAN MAKE FOR
Valentine's Day

31

VALENTINE HEART ART

SKILL LEVEL

TIME

SUPPLIES

- ☐ 10 by 10-inch canvas
- ☐ white paper
- ☐ graphite paper
- ☐ heart silhouette
- ☐ raised letter stickers
- ☐ white craft paint
- ☐ gold paint pen

Westleigh says...

You can also spell out a special Valentine's message, such as "Be My Valentine."

Whitney says...

You can also paint the canvas to match your room.

INSTRUCTIONS

1. Turn to the template on page 141 and trace a heart onto a sheet of white paper.

2. Using the graphite paper, trace the heart outline onto the square canvas.

3. Place the stickers along the traced outline, spelling out "Best Friends Forever and Ever."

4. Paint the entire canvas with the white craft paint.

5. Let dry.

6. Using the gold paint pen, trace the tops of the letters with gold paint. Your valentine is ready!

Step 2

Step 3

Step 4

Step 6

32

VALENTINE FELT HEART PILLOW

SKILL LEVEL

TIME

SUPPLIES

- [ ] white pillow cover
- [ ] pillow form
- [ ] red felt
- [ ] fabric pen
- [ ] craft glue
- [ ] white paint pen

Done!

INSTRUCTIONS

1. Trace the large and small heart patterns on page 141 onto a piece of paper.

2. Cut out the hearts.

3. Place the hearts on the red felt and trace 12 large hearts and 12 small hearts with a fabric pen.

4. Cut out the hearts.

5. Trace "faux stitches" around the edges of the hearts with the white paint pen.

6. Let dry.

7. Place the hearts in a random pattern on the pillow cover.

8. Glue the hearts in place with fabric glue.

9. Let dry.

10. Insert the pillow form into the pillow cover and zip it shut.

Step 2

Step 5

33

TASSEL HEART NECKLACE

SKILL LEVEL

TIME

SUPPLIES

- [ ] white leather
- [ ] small hole punch
- [ ] leather cord
- [ ] pencil
- [ ] white embroidery thread
- [ ] gold jump rings

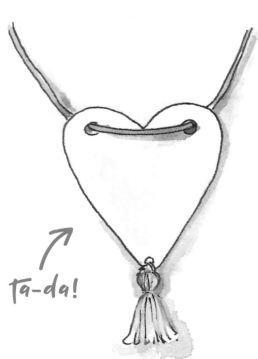

Ta-da!

INSTRUCTIONS

1. Turn to page 141 and trace the large heart pattern onto a piece of paper.

2. Cut out the heart.

3. Place the heart on the white leather and trace around it with a pencil. Cut out the heart.

4. Punch two holes in the top of the heart and one hole in the bottom of the heart.

5. Turn to page 138 and follow the instructions to make a tassel from white embroidery thread.

6. Trim the tassel and insert a jump ring in the top.

7. Insert another jump ring into the hole at the bottom of the heart.

8. Link the two jump rings together.

9. String a piece of leather cord through the two holes at the top of the heart and tie off the necklace to the length you want.

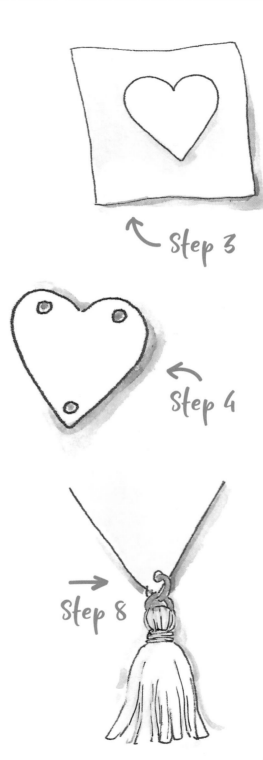

Step 3

Step 4

Step 8

34

VALENTINE HEART BOUQUET

SKILL LEVEL

TIME

SUPPLIES

- [ ] large round glass vase
- [ ] smaller round glass vase that fits inside the larger one
- [ ] flowers
- [ ] water
- [ ] candy hearts

INSTRUCTIONS

1. Place the smaller vase inside the larger vase.

2. Fill the area between the 2 vases with conversation hearts.

3. Fill the small vase with water. Arrange the flowers in the smaller vase.

4. Your heart bouquet is ready to display!

Step 1

Step 2

← Sweet!

STUFF YOU CAN MAKE FOR

Easter

35

JUTE TWINE NEST

SKILL LEVEL

TIME

SUPPLIES

- [ ] jute twine
- [ ] craft glue
- [ ] water
- [ ] plastic wrap
- [ ] 2 bowls (one for mixing and one for a form)
- [ ] scissors

INSTRUCTIONS

1. Mix 3 parts water to 1 part glue in a bowl. Mix them thoroughly until combined.

2. Cut 15 pieces of twine 6 inches long.

3. Cut 15 pieces of twine 4 inches long.

4. Flip the remaining bowl over. This is your form. Cover it with a piece of plastic wrap.

5. Dip one of the pieces of 6-inch twine into the glue/water mixture. Let it soak until it is completely saturated.

6. Place the piece of twine on the bowl.

7. Repeat step 5 and 6 with another piece of twine crossing over the first.

8. Keep dipping and placing the twine on the bowl form until you have completely covered the top of the bowl, creating a nest.

9. Let dry.

10. Remove the nest from the plastic and the bowl and flip it right side up.

11. Trim the edges.

12. Fill the nest with straw and put some paper eggs inside for Easter.

Step 10

So cute!

36

CHALKBOARD WORD-FIND EGGS

SKILL LEVEL

TIME

SUPPLIES

- [ ] wood eggs
- [ ] chalkboard paint
- [ ] brush
- [ ] fine-tipped chalk marker

Westleigh says...

If I'm giving the egg to a friend, I try to include words of things they like.

Whitney says...

I like to give the eggs with a box of chalk wrapped up with a bow.

INSTRUCTIONS

1. Paint the eggs with chalkboard paint.

2. Let dry. Add a second coat if necessary.

3. Pick four short words you want your friends to find.

4. With the fine-tipped chalkboard marker, write the words on the egg with one letter connecting each word to another.

5. Fill in the rest of the spaces with random letters.

6. Give the egg to a friend for Easter and let them solve the puzzle.

Step 1

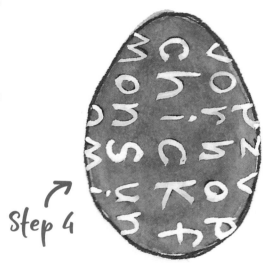

Step 4

← Done!

37

FABRIC BUNNY PILLOW

SKILL LEVEL

TIME

SUPPLIES

- [ ] 1 yard lightweight cotton fabric
- [ ] fabric glue
- [ ] fabric pen
- [ ] Poly-fil stuffing
- [ ] yarn
- [ ] cardboard
- [ ] scissors

← Adorable!

INSTRUCTIONS

1 Turn to page 142. Trace the bunny silhouette onto a piece of white paper and cut it out.

2 Place the bunny on the fabric. Trace it with a fabric pen and cut it out.

3 Flip the bunny over. Place it on the fabric, trace it with a fabric pen, and cut it out.

4 On the wrong side of the fabric of one of the bunny silhouettes, place a line of glue all around the edges, leaving a 4-inch opening at the bottom.

5 Place the other bunny silhouette on top so the 2 wrong sides of the fabric are together and the 2 right sides of the fabric are on the outside.

6 Once the bunny silhouettes are dry, stuff with Poly-fil stuffing.

7 Glue the opening closed.

8 Turn to page 137 and follow the instructions to make a small pom-pom. Use a 2-inch piece of cardboard.

9 Once your pom-pom is finished, glue it to the back of the bunny.

Step 2

Step 4

38

WOOD EASTER BLOCKS

SKILL LEVEL

TIME

SUPPLIES

- ☐ 4 unfinished wood blocks from a craft store
- ☐ pink craft paint
- ☐ white craft paint
- ☐ craft glue
- ☐ paintbrush
- ☐ Q-tip
- ☐ chipboard letters

Westleigh says...

You could try stripes instead of polka dots or both!

Whitney says...

I like to spell out other words, such as EASTER or JOY or SPRING or HAPPY.

INSTRUCTIONS

1. Paint two of the blocks with pink craft paint, and paint two of the blocks with white craft paint. Let them dry.

2. Using a Q-tip or paintbrush, add white polka dots to the pink blocks and pink polka dots to the white blocks. Let dry.

3. Glue chipboard letters that spell NEST onto the front of the blocks.

4. Your blocks are ready to decorate for Easter.

Step 1 ↘

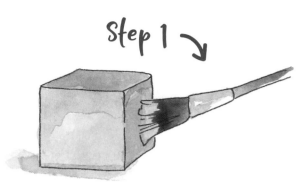

Step 2

↖ lovely!

STUFF YOU CAN MAKE FOR THE

Fourth of July

39

PATRIOTIC RIBBON BANNER

SKILL LEVEL

TIME

SUPPLIES

- [ ] 2 rolls of blue-and-white polka-dot ribbon
- [ ] 2 rolls of red-and-white striped ribbon
- [ ] 2 rolls of blue-and-white checked ribbon
- [ ] 2 rolls of red-and-white polka-dot ribbon
- [ ] jute twine
- [ ] scissors

INSTRUCTIONS

1. Cut 12 pieces of blue-and-white polka-dot ribbon 12 inches long.

2. Cut 12 pieces of red-and-white-striped ribbon 12 inches long.

3. Cut 12 pieces of red-and-white polka-dot ribbon 12 inches long.

4. Cut 12 pieces of blue-and-white-checked ribbon 12 inches long.

5. Cut a piece of jute twine 36 inches long.

6. Start approximately 4 inches from the end of the twine and loop one of the ribbons over the twine in half.

7. Tie a knot on the twine in the center of the ribbon so there are now two streamers created from one ribbon.

8. Select another piece of ribbon in a different pattern and repeat step 7.

9. Keep tying ribbons to the twine in alternating patterns until you have tied them all. Your banner is ready for the Fourth of July!

Steps 1–5

Step 8

40

BANDANA PILLOW

SKILL LEVEL

TIME

SUPPLIES

- ☐ 1 red bandana
- ☐ 1 blue bandana
- ☐ pillow form

Westleigh says...

You don't have to use red and blue just because it's the Fourth of July. I like white and pink for my room.

Whitney says...

You can always make extras for friends.

INSTRUCTIONS

1. Place one red bandana flat on a table. Press smooth to remove any wrinkles.

2. Place a pillow form on top of the bandana.

3. Place the blue bandana on top of the pillow form to create a bandana sandwich with the pillow in the center.

4. Tie a knot at one corner.

5. Tie a knot at each of the other three corners. Your pillow is ready to decorate with!

Step 1

Love it!

41

FOURTH OF JULY BRAIDED BRACELET

SKILL LEVEL

TIME

SUPPLIES

- [ ] chunky red yarn
- [ ] chunky blue yarn
- [ ] chunky white yarn
- [ ] scissors

↖ Step 8

INSTRUCTIONS

1. Cut a 10-inch piece of red yarn.

2. Cut a 10-inch piece of blue yarn.

3. Cut a 10-inch piece of white yarn.

4. Tie the three pieces of yarn together with one knot at the end.

5. Braid the pieces to the other end and tie a knot.

6. Repeat steps 1 through 5 to make a second braid.

7. Repeat steps 1 through 5 to make a third braid.

8. Tie the three braided strands together with one knot at the end.

9. Braid the pieces to the other end and tie a knot.

10. Wrap the finished braid around your wrist to make sure it fits.

11. Tie off the end to complete your bracelet. It might be fun to make another one for a friend!

Steps 1–3

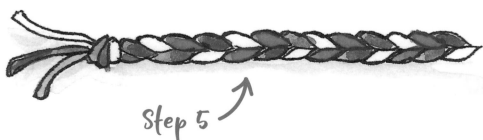

Step 5

42

FIRECRACKER PARTY POPPERS

SKILL LEVEL

TIME

SUPPLIES

- [ ] paper-towel rolls
- [ ] confetti
- [ ] white twist ties
- [ ] blue-and-white striped tissue paper
- [ ] red-and-white striped tissue paper
- [ ] scissors

INSTRUCTIONS

1. Cut a paper-towel roll in half and set it on a piece of tissue paper.

2. Fill the center of the paper-towel roll with confetti.

3. Wrap up the paper-towel holder in the tissue paper.

4. Secure the end with a white twist tie. Your poppers are ready to party!

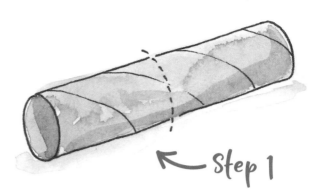

← Step 1

Step 2

Party time!

Westleigh says...
My family opens our poppers every year—they are so much fun!

Whitney says...
You could also include your favorite jokes or Scripture verses or quotes on little pieces of paper inside the poppers with the confetti.

STUFF YOU CAN MAKE FOR

Thanksgiving

43

THANKFUL TREE

SKILL LEVEL

TIME

SUPPLIES

- [ ] branches
- [ ] construction paper
- [ ] hole punch
- [ ] jute twine
- [ ] markers
- [ ] small rocks
- [ ] urn or vase

Sweet!

INSTRUCTIONS

1. Find branches from your yard. Clean them off and remove any leaves.

2. Turn to page 143. Trace the leaf template onto pieces of construction paper and cut out the leaves.

3. Have each family member write things they are thankful for on each leaf with a marker.

4. Punch a hole in the end of each leaf and thread a small piece of jute twine through the hole.

5. Fill the urn or vase with small rocks or pebbles.

6. Place the branches in the urn or vase.

7. Tie the leaves to the branches. This makes a wonderful Thanksgiving centerpiece and a great reminder of all that we have to be thankful for.

Step 1

Step 2

Step 4

Westleigh says...
I am thankful for my mom.

Whitney says...
I am thankful for my family.

44

FELT AND LEATHER LEAF GARLAND

SKILL LEVEL

TIME

SUPPLIES

- ☐ thick gray felt
- ☐ white felt
- ☐ mini hole punch
- ☐ leather strip
- ☐ pencil

Westleigh says...

I like to use my garland to decorate the bookshelf in my room.

Whitney says...

I like to hang my garland over a picture on the wall.

INSTRUCTIONS

1. Turn to the template on page 143. Trace the leaves onto paper and cut them out.

2. Use a pencil to trace around the paper leaves onto the felt.

3. Cut out the felt leaves. You will need 25 to 30 leaves for this project.

4. Punch two holes in the middle of each leaf with the small hole punch.

5. Cut a piece of leather cord 36 inches long.

6. Thread the leather cord through the middle of the leaf and knot the end.

7. Continue threading the leaves through the cord, mixing up smaller and larger leaves as you go.

8. Once all the leaves are threaded, tie off the other end of the leather cord. Your garland is ready to use for a decoration!

Step 1

Step 4

Step 5

Fabulous!

45

PINE CONE AND LEAF THANKSGIVING PLACE CARDS

SKILL LEVEL

TIME

SUPPLIES

- [ ] faux fall leaves
- [ ] pine cones
- [ ] gold paint pen

Done!

INSTRUCTIONS

1. Write each guest's name on a leaf.

2. Decorate the leaf with polka dots or doodles.

3. Place a pine cone at each setting.

4. Tuck the leaf into the edges of the pine cone. Each guest now has a personalized place setting and a small gift to take away from the Thanksgiving table!

Step 1

Step 2

46

FABRIC PUMPKINS

SKILL LEVEL

TIME

SUPPLIES

- [ ] fabric
- [ ] pencil
- [ ] needle
- [ ] thread
- [ ] stuffing
- [ ] florist wire
- [ ] fabric glue

Finito!

INSTRUCTIONS

1. Spread out your fabric facedown.

2. Place a small plate on the fabric. Trace around it with a pencil on the backside of the fabric and cut it out.

3. Flip over your fabric and trim away any stray threads.

4. Turn to page 134 to learn how to create a straight stitch. Stich a small hem around the edge of the fabric with a straight stitch.

5. Flip the circle inside out.

6. Place the wire inside the hem and pull until you have a small hole.

7. Stuff the inside of your pumpkin with enough stuffing to fill up the pumpkin.

8. Once the pumpkin is stuffed, pull the wire until the opening is closed.

9. Twist the ends of the wire together.

10. Cut leaves out of fabric. Using fabric glue, attach the leaves to the top of the pumpkin.

Step 4 →

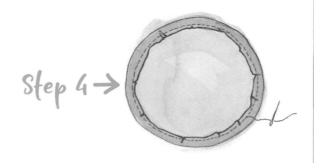

← Step 6

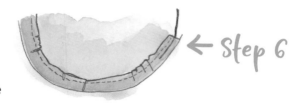

Step 7 →

Step 10

47

MINI PINE CONE WREATHS

SKILL LEVEL

TIME

SUPPLIES

- [ ] mini pine cones
- [ ] cardboard
- [ ] scissors
- [ ] glue
- [ ] ribbon

Westleigh says...

I like to hang my wreath over a picture frame.

Whitney says...

I like to make two wreaths and hang them on either side of my door.

INSTRUCTIONS

1. Cut out a 6-inch cardboard circle.

2. Trace a 3-inch circle in the center of the 6-inch circle. Cut out the smaller circle, creating a wreath form.

3. Glue a small pine cone to the cardboard.

4. Continue gluing pine cones to the cardboard until the entire wreath is covered.

5. Once the wreath is dry, tie a ribbon around the center and hang up the wreath.

← Step 3

Done!

STUFF YOU CAN MAKE FOR

Christmas

48

NATIVITY WREATH

SKILL LEVEL

TIME

SUPPLIES

- [ ] small grapevine wreath
- [ ] small traditional wood clothespin
- [ ] 4 by 6-inch square of white cotton
- [ ] straw
- [ ] glue
- [ ] ribbon

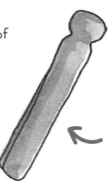

INSTRUCTIONS

1. Place the small clothespin in the center of the piece of cotton.

2. Wrap the cotton around the clothespin like a blanket and glue in place.

3. Glue the pieces of straw to the bottom of the wreath.

4. Let dry.

5. Glue the "clothespin baby Jesus" wrapped in cotton to the center of the straw.

6. Let dry.

7. Wrap a ribbon through the center of the top of the wreath and hang the wreath.

Step 1

Step 2

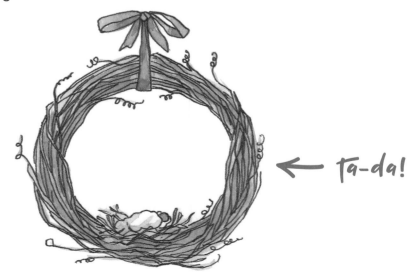

Ta-da!

49

GLITTER CHRISTMAS TREE ORNAMENTS

SKILL LEVEL

TIME

SUPPLIES

- [ ] popsicle sticks
- [ ] scissors
- [ ] paintbrush
- [ ] glue
- [ ] glitter
- [ ] mini wood stars
- [ ] ribbon

Cute!

INSTRUCTIONS

1. Select three popsicle sticks. Cut one slightly shorter than the other two with scissors and set aside the rest of the piece you cut off (this will be used later as your trunk).

Step 1 ↗

2. Place all three popsicle sticks in the shape of a triangle, using the longer two popsicle sticks as the sides and the shorter popsicle stick as the base.

3. Glue the stars around the edge of the popsicle stick Christmas tree.

4. Glue the part of the popsicle stick you cut off to the bottom as a trunk.

Step 2 ↗

5. Let the popsicle sticks and the stars dry.

6. Brush the tree and stars with glue.

7. Sprinkle glitter.

8. Cut a piece of ribbon and thread it through the top of the tree.

9. Tie a knot in the ribbon and hang your ornament on your tree.

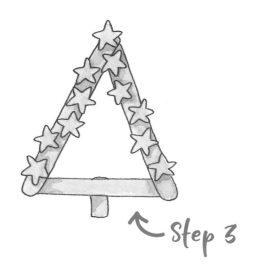

↖ Step 3

50

MINI PIPE-CLEANER SNOWFLAKES

SKILL LEVEL

TIME

SUPPLIES

- ☐ 25 cream pipe cleaners
- ☐ scissors
- ☐ ribbon

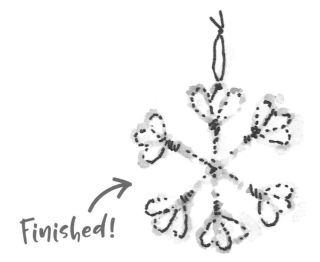

Finished!

INSTRUCTIONS

1. Lay three pipe cleaners one over another in a star pattern.

2. Twist them all together in the middle to form a star with six prongs.

3. Twist another pipe cleaner into three loops, leaving a tail.

4. Repeat step 3 with five more pipe cleaners.

5. Wire one of the looped pipe cleaners to the end of each of the prongs of the star using the tail.

6. Tie a piece of ribbon, fluff the pipe cleaners, and your snowflake is ready to hang on the tree or decorate a package.

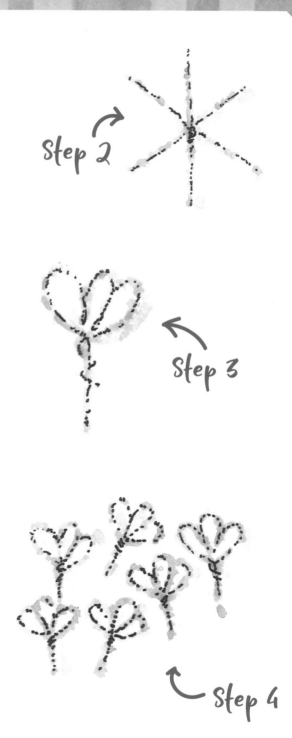

Step 2

Step 3

Step 4

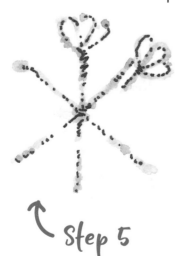

Step 5

51

SNOWDROP POM-POM ORNAMENTS

SKILL LEVEL

TIME

SUPPLIES

- [ ] white chunky yarn
- [ ] cardboard
- [ ] ribbon
- [ ] scissors

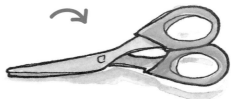

INSTRUCTIONS

1. Turn to page 137 and follow the instruction to make medium-sized pom-poms with a 4-inch piece of cardboard. Use chunky yarn to make your pom-poms extra fluffy.

2. Leave a long tail when you tie the string around the center of the yarn to make the pom-pom.

3. Tie the tail together to create a loop. Tie a bow on the loop.

4. Fluff and trim your pom-poms until they are round.

5. Use the loop to hang your ornaments on the tree.

Step 3

Too cute!

52

BRAIDED PINE CONE GARLAND

SKILL LEVEL

TIME

SUPPLIES

- [ ] white yarn
- [ ] mini pine cones
- [ ] scissors

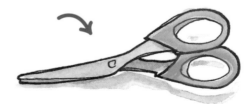

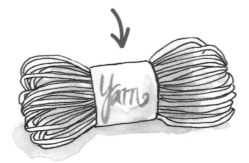

INSTRUCTIONS

1. Cut three pieces of yarn 36 inches long.

2. Braid the pieces together into one long strand. (Tie the ends onto something stationary before you start. This will make the braiding much easier.)

3. Tie off both ends of the braid.

4. Glue the mini pine cones onto the braid every 4 inches.

5. Let dry. Your garland is ready to use to decorate with!

HOW TO SEW STITCHES

Running Stitch

This is the most basic of all the stitches. Push the needle from the bottom of the fabric up through the top. Pull tight. Following a straight line, measure approximately ½ inch and push the needle through the fabric from the top to the bottom. Leave another ½-inch gap and push the needle back through the fabric from the bottom to the top. Repeat this process until you have enough stitches for the project. When you're finished, you'll have a straight line of ½-inch stitches with ½-inch gaps. It will look like it's "running" across the fabric.

Straight Stitch

This stitch is like the running stitch but without the gap between the stitches. Push the needle from the bottom of the fabric up through the top. Pull tight. Following a straight line, measure approximately ½ inch and push the needle through the fabric from the top to the bottom. Go back to where your original stitch ends and push the needle back through the fabric from the bottom to the top. Repeat this process until you have enough stitches for your project. When you're finished, you will have a series of ½-inch stitches next to each other without gaps.

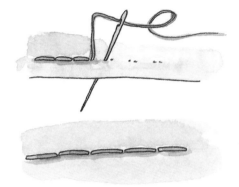

Backstitch

Push the needle from the bottom of the fabric up through the top. Pull tight and then push the needle back through the fabric to create a ½-inch stitch. Next, measure approximately 1 inch from the first stitch and thread the needle up through the fabric. Pull tight, go back to the end of your first stitch, and thread the needle right next to the original stitch. Then, simply repeat until you have the amount of stitches needed for the project. When finished, this stitch will be a straight line of tight, ½-inch stitches. This stitch looks pretty from both sides of the fabric.

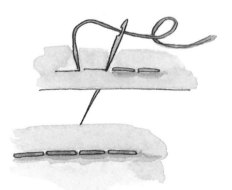

Satin Stitch

You use this stitch when you want to fill in an area on your embroidery pattern. Following the outline you've sketched on your embroidery (or notebook), start at one end and pull the needle from the bottom of the fabric up through the top. Stitch across the design you are filling and reinsert the needle on the other side. Then, simply repeat until you have filled in the design. When you're finished, this stitch creates a solid, filled-in area on the embroidery.

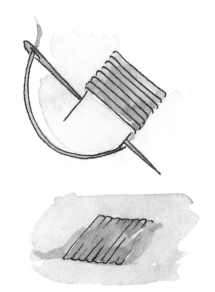

Blanket Stitch

Tie a knot in the end of your thread. Pull the needle from the bottom of the fabric up through the top about ¼ inch from the edge of the fabric. Pull tight, wrap the thread around the edge of the material, and then pull the needle back up through the fabric (in the same place) to create the first stitch. Next, measure approximately ¼ inch from the first stitch (also ¼ inch from the edge of the fabric) and thread the needle up through the fabric. Wrap the thread around the edge of the material and then pull the needle back through, just like the first stitch—but this time, thread the needle through the center of the thread, creating a loop. Pull the thread tightly until you have a stitch that runs across the top of the fabric. Then simply repeat until you have the number of stitches needed for the project. When finished, this stitch will create a running border along the edge of the fabric.

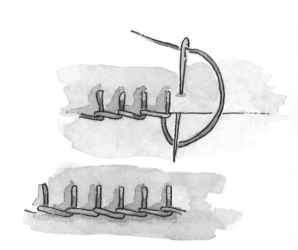

HOW TO MAKE POM-POMS

1. Start by wrapping yarn around a cardboard rectangle at least 45 times. The size of the piece of cardboard will determine the size of the pom-pom. And the more yarn you wrap around the cardboard, the thicker your pom-pom will be.

2. Gently slide the yarn off the cardboard and cut another piece of yarn approximately 10 inches long. Place your wrapped yarn on the 10-inch piece of yarn.

3. Tie the 10-inch piece of yarn around the center of your wrapped yarn. Tie it tightly and then tie it again. We don't want your pom-pom coming loose!

4. Clip the loops of your pom-pom with scissors. Fluff the pom-pom and trim it until you have something that resembles a round pom-pom. (This is the fun part.) Be careful not to give it too much of a haircut, or your pom-pom will simply be a small pom instead!

5. Repeat the steps until you have enough pom-poms for your project. Compare the pom-poms to each other as you make them to keep them all about the same size.

Step 1

Step 2

Step 3

Step 4

Pretty!

HOW TO MAKE TASSELS

1. Start by wrapping yarn around a cardboard rectangle at least 45 times. The size of the piece of cardboard will determine the size of the tassel. And the more yarn you wrap around the cardboard, the thicker your tassel will be.

Step 1

2. Cut two pieces of yarn approximately 10 inches long.

3. Thread one of the pieces between the loops of yarn and the cardboard and tie it off, leaving the strings hanging. This is the piece you will use to attach your tassel to something, such as a garland.

Step 3

4. Gently slide the loops of yarn off the cardboard.

← Step 4

5. Tie the second 10-inch piece of yarn around the outside of your wrapped yarn, 1 inch from the top.

6. Tie it tightly, tie it again, and trim the ends.

7. Then simply clip the loops of your tassel with scissors.

8. Repeat the steps until you have enough tassels for your project. Compare the tassels to each other as you go to keep them all about the same size.

Step 5

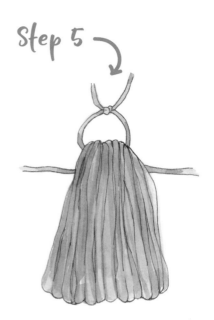

Fabulous!

HOW TO USE MOD PODGE

Use Mod Podge to adhere one surface to another quickly and easily. It can be a little sticky. Literally. Here are some easy tips and tricks to using Mod Podge.

1. Use a sponge brush or a flat brush for easy application. Apply the Mod Podge to both pieces you are sticking together.

2. When applying Mod Podge to a surface, make sure you cover the area completely. This will prevent wrinkles. If you don't coat the entire surface with Mod Podge, the two pieces won't stick together properly.

3. Press the two pieces together. Use a roller on the top piece to prevent any bubbles from forming between them. The more time you take smoothing out the surface, the fewer bubbles you will have on your project.

4. Mod Podge dries quickly, so don't apply too much at one time, especially if you are working on a large surface. Each coat will dry in 15 to 20 minutes.

5. In addition to using like a glue, you can spread Mod Podge over your project to create a nice finish. Most projects need about two coats of Mod Podge. Make sure to let each coat dry thoroughly before you coat the next one.

TEMPLATES

Small Heart

Large Heart

Bunny 2

leaves

To Mama:

*The one who inspires us, encourages us,
and is always there to listen.*

Thank you for believing in us.

We love you more.

Cover design by Nicole Dougherty

Interior design by Faceout Studio

Grid lines behind craft titles © xnova / Shutterstock

Published in association with the William K. Jensen Literary Agency, 119 Bampton Court, Eugene, Oregon 97404.

HARVEST KIDS is a trademark of The Hawkins Children's LLC. Harvest House Publishers, Inc., is the exclusive licensee of the trademark HARVEST KIDS.

52 DIY Crafts for Girls

Artwork © 2020 by Michal Sparks

Published by Harvest House Publishers

Eugene, Oregon 97408

www.harvesthousepublishers.com

ISBN 978-0-7369-7408-0 (pbk.)

Library of Congress Cataloging-in-Publication Data record is available at https://lccn.loc.gov/2019028496

Printed in China

19 20 21 22 23 24 25 26 27 28 / RDS-FO / 10 9 8 7 6 5 4 3 2 1